CRISIS OVER RHODESIA:
A SKEPTICAL VIEW

Studies in International Affairs Number 3

Studies in International Affairs Number 3

CRISIS OVER RHODESIA: A SKEPTICAL VIEW

by Charles Burton Marshall

Washington Center of Foreign Policy Research
School of Advanced International Studies
The Johns Hopkins University

The Johns Hopkins Press, Baltimore, Maryland

FOREWORD

A striking feature of international politics since World War II has been the emergence and political mobilization of new states in the underdeveloped areas of the world, especially in Africa. The complexity of this development—the confused clash of traditional and modernizing influences; the interaction of racial, tribal, and personal conflicts with incipient nationalism—has defied both the great expectations of a new order for the developing nations and the fears of an ever-expanding chaos. Nonetheless, the great liberal states continue to feel compelled (by conscience and by the desire to gain the good opinion of the underdeveloped world) to avow the great expectations, even if they are privately disillusioned. In this circumstance the persistence of thriving governments in which white men rule and enjoy a privileged status on a self-consciously non-white continent seems like a troublesome anomaly left over from a varnished past. Anomalous or not, this phenomenon is an important reality with hard consequences for all states that want to influence developments in Africa. It is a reality that does not yield to policies and postures that neglect the limits of statecraft.

On the other hand, it is just as important to take account of the human elements of the problem as it is to be hard-headed about the realities of power and influence. It is incumbent upon responsible men and governments to appreciate the tragic complexity of the moral issues in countries like Rhodesia as well as the entanglement of these issues with considerations of national interest, whether they are primary considerations or products of international opinion.

Consistent with the Washington Center's interest in the practical and moral implications for international politics of the changing scene in underdeveloped areas, Charles Burton Marshall in this essay reflects upon the peculiar problems of Rhodesia's internal and international status. He distinguishes and analyzes the major components of the Rhodesian crisis—"if it is a crisis"—against a background of relevant facts, so that the issues of principle, humanity, and statecraft can be more fully comprehended. This is a particularly useful service because relevant data and intellectual clarity about Rhodesia have been conspicuously lacking in the public media and in the U.N.'s deliberations.

This is the third publication in the Center's new booklet series, Studies in International Affairs.

March 1967

ROBERT E. OSGOOD
Director
Washington Center of
Foreign Policy Research

CONTENTS

CRISIS OVER RHODESIA:
A SKEPTICAL VIEW

Studies in International Affairs Number 3

INTRODUCTION: WHY THIS ESSAY?

Babble, babble; our old England may go down in babble at last.
—Lord Tennyson

My interest in the crisis—if it is a crisis—over Rhodesia during its earlier phases was mainly that of a person habituated to scanning, clipping, and filing news items about international problems arising in whatever locality. During brief travel in Southern Africa in the spring of 1966, however, I became aware of aspects which would ordinarily elude anyone dependent on mass media for his grasp of the situation. From close by, I saw Rhodesia in a different perspective. An experience in the late autumn of 1966 deepened my concern.

At that time the Security Council was about to consider a proposal to invoke, for the first time ever, compulsory coercive commercial restrictions purportedly to save the international peace from a miscreant's threat. The Charter's phrase for such a venture is "interruption of economic relations." The pejorative term is boycott. The flattering word is sanctions, flattering because of its suggestion of sacredness. That hinted quality affords a façade for havoc, disruption, deprivation, and stimulus for civil violence in other people's lands—the operational realities of the idea. The usage enables officials to propose and to plan such things with much piety and self-congratulation. I have often heard devout men endorse sanctions, men who would blanch in horror at the thought of advocating a hostile design for large-scale starvation among a people whom they do not know and who probably have done them no harm. The United States had signified an intention to go along with the idea of sanctions against Rhodesia.

On the occasion in point, I heard a State Department hierarch answer relevant questions. A doubter put a query: How, in actuality, was the purported miscreant, Rhodesia, threatening the peace? The answer came: Obviously, the United States could not condone the situation there. The inquirer persisted: What country was Rhodesia presumably about to attack? The answer: Not precisely any country; the situation was subtler than that, some of Rhodesia's neighbors were acutely unhappy about it, and Rhodesia moreover was in rebellion against the Crown, a sort of thing that could not be accepted. A third question: Wherein precisely was Rhodesia in rebellion? The answer: The British government had left no room for doubt about the matter, and so it would be pointless to go into technicalities.

Sanctions and boycotts are hostile undertakings. In my view, the basis for the United States to join in action of such character should be more precise and substantial than what had been indicated. Anyway, an argument against getting technical would probably arouse my suspicion in any context. It is only by a respect for technicalities that we can keep our thinking rigorous, and only by rigorous thinking that we can manage to know what we are doing in great affairs. In particular, for me, the asserted unacceptability of rebellion against the Crown was not a compelling argument. The city in which the dialogue was occurring honored the name of a President who had endeared himself to his countrymen by leading such a rebellion, and his next five successors in the American presidency also had parts in it.

I felt constrained to a more active curiosity. Accordingly, I paid close heed as the subsequent proceedings unfolded in the Security Council.

The record of relevant debate in that body proved not very illuminating. The participants' statements were assertive rather than analytic. Along with presenting a hope and a formula for doing "the greatest economic damage" to Rhodesia, the British spokesman referred to "the great moral issue" involved. That thought was echoed all around, but no one did more than declare the morality of it all. The persistent protests of moral intent set my mind to wondering about the practicalities. It also reminded me of Edmund Burke's phrase about "the delusive plausibilities of moral politicians." My reaction was not the cynical one of dismissing the relevance of morality to high policy. It was a case of being alerted by the flaunting of an abstraction calculated to foreclose argument, to pre-empt the conclusion, and to abjure compromise. Morality in large affairs imposes many obligations, among them an obligation to entertain the possibility of there being some measure of right on either side in a dispute and at least to avoid judgment in such a matter without first hearing more than one view of the merits.

The regime in Rhodesia was repeatedly described as consisting of usurpers. Nobody mentioned the fact of its achievement of office through elections held in pursuance of British law.

The United Kingdom was referred to recurringly as the "administering power" over Rhodesia. This phrase struck me as an especially interesting instance of language that not merely obscured but indeed inverted meaning. There would be no problem, hence no issue, if the United Kingdom were indeed the administering power, or had administering power, respecting Rhodesia. In that situation, it would have only to issue an order, which ipso facto would take effect. In fact, Britain was not in that position. Rhodesia was not in the complementary position. This was not and indeed, as I would learn, never had been the relationship between them.

A spokesman for one of the governments represented at the Security Council referred to a question of logical compatibility between the concept of a concern domestic to British jurisdiction and the notion of the issue as being a responsibility for a world community, a topic appealing to logical imagination. Thereupon he declared the two propositions to be compatible—QED—but disappointingly he left the thought undemonstrated.

The assumption regarding a threat to the peace, such as to qualify the problem for consideration under the Charter provision being invoked, was dealt with variously. According to a postulate applied by the Security Council thirteen months previously, the situation in Rhodesia, if prolonged, might generate such a threat. Now, one participant adverted to that declaratory hypothesis. The situation had been prolonged, he added. Ipso facto it had become a threat, he concluded. Several other spokesmen averred the growing menace to be obvious. To clinch the point, one declared that only the blind and deaf could miss the portents.

Beyond such declaratory arguments, the Security Council's record for the period of December 8–16, 1966, afforded little on the propriety of considering

the problem under Chapter VII of the Charter referring to threats to the peace, breaches of the peace,
and acts of aggression. Concerning the roots of the
issue, moreover, the record revealed virtually nothing. I turned back to the Security Council's earlier
deliberations, first in November, 1965, when it had
called for a voluntary boycott to head off a pre-
sumptive incipient threat to the peace and then in
April, 1966, when it authorized the British to use
force at sea if necessary to interdict oil shipments
specifically destined for Rhodesia via Mozambique.
Here again the record gave little light on the gen-
esis and nature of the issues.

To counter doubts concerning the propriety of
mandatory sanctions, the United States Ambassador
to the United Nations has said, "I must point out
that it is the explicit prerogative of the Security
Council under Article 39 of the United Nations
Charter to make a finding that there is a threat to
international peace and security. In the case of
Rhodesia, the Security Council has reviewed the
facts of the case and made precisely such a determination." The first element is like dismissing a
criticism of a pie by remarking that a baker made it.
The second element, in which the Ambassador claims
judicial thoroughness and conclusiveness for the
processes by which the decision was arrived at, involves a qualitative appraisal of the deliberations.
My own appraisal is sharply at variance with the
Ambassador's. Anyone relying on what the Security
Council has adduced for comprehension of the problem would know all too little for informed judgment.

Unsatisfied curiosity impelled me to review the
bulging packet of clippings in my files. They proved
more revealing than the Security Council's delibera-

tions, but the aggregate fell short of a full and co-
herent account. Next I perused a half-dozen or so
histories and monographs. Then I checked through
background documents. All this passing effort has
not made me an expert on Rhodesia's past or present, but I feel somewhat better posted on the background of what the United States Ambassador,
quoted above, has properly called "an extremely
important matter."

Its importance gives promise of increasing. In
prospect is a fair chance of failure of mandatory
sanctions to achieve the designed goal of inflicting
havoc and agony enough to bring down the regime.
If and as that failure becomes increasingly evident,
the Security Council will be pressed to take further
steps along the course set forth in the Charter, Article 42, which reads: "Should the Security Council
consider that measures provided for in Article 41 . . .
have proved to be inadequate, it may take such action
by air, sea, or land forces as may be necessary to
maintain or restore international peace or security.
Such action may include demonstrations, blockade,
and other operations by air, sea, or land forces of
Members of the United Nations." Whom the finger
will be on then is clear enough. Having once concurred in deeming the Rhodesia problem to be within
the compass of Chapter VII of the Charter, our
magistrates may find it difficult to reason out an ex-
cuse for resisting the importunities.

A better informed public may serve both to check
and to help our magistrates. With this thought in
mind, I decided to set down in brief form what I had
learned about the roots and character of the Rhodesian issue.

II. THE ROOTS OF AN ISSUE

Britain until recently encouraged them for nearly 40 years to think of themselves more as a self-governing dominion than as the Crown Colony to which it is trying to reduce Rhodesia at the moment.—Laurens van der Post

The issue between the United Kingdom and Rhodesia whence has arisen the crisis before the United Nations has an institutional and constitutional background. To appraise the issue one must understand that background. It is not enough merely to accept at face value opprobrious labels applied to the Rhodesian regime. The debates on Rhodesia within the Security Council have been as singularly deficient in information about that background as they have been replete with such labels. Unfortunately, the pronouncements by which spokesmen for the United States government have sought to explain United States support of the British position have been similarly unreflective. The purpose of this chapter is, in brief narrative, to relate the background.

The prehistoric phases of human activity in the area called Rhodesia run back many hundreds of millenia. The history encompasses a little more than a hundred years. The portion essential to this account dates back seventy-eight years. Its initial stage is linked with the character and ambitions of the man from whom the land derived its name.

In 1889 Cecil John Rhodes was in his mid-thirties. English by birth, he had migrated in youth to the Cape Colony in what is now the Republic of South Africa. By dint of work, luck, and perhaps genius, he became a directing spirit there. According to biographers, his was "a giant personality"—crude, naïve, and domineering, but also magnanimous. Though frail, he had extraordinary energy and a predisposition toward large designs. His most spacious notion was a dream of establishing a domain, under British aegis, running the length of Africa from Egypt to the Cape as a counterpart to the Crown's other imperium across the Indian Ocean. He affirmed for the British Crown a civilizing mission. He did not hold every culture to be as good as every other, but he regarded all breeds of men as equal in potential. He envisioned a polity based on standards and practices of white men's culture at its best, according to his understanding, and with people of every pigmentation eventually eligible to share in it equally.

Impatient of bureaucracy, Rhodes projected imperial schemes on a precept of the less governmental direction, the better. "Give me a free hand and leave it to me to secure all that can be secured" was his plea in seeking authorization in London to make a venture from the Cape, via Bechuanaland, into lands north of the Limpopo River not yet claimed by any power, but exposed to pre-emption by the Boer Republic in the Transvaal or perhaps by some European state. Increments of native labor for the Cape might be recruited there. Precious metals might be found, along with the satisfaction of settling new territory. Rhodes' associates in a joint-stock development enterprise called the British South Africa Company already held an ambiguous concession marked by an indigenous ruler's X.

The British government of the time, while not averse to expansion, was reluctant to put up money or men—an attitude congenial to Rhodes' plans. In London he used his prestige to win over the Queen and important blocs in the House of Commons, whose approval was necessary. He returned to Cape Town with a royal charter vesting quasisovereign authority in the company for twenty-five years. It could make treaties, receive concessions, maintain forces for security and order, administer justice, and create and operate public works. The device was familiar to colonial enterprises of an earlier epoch in America and India.

With considerable autonomy, the company would be in effect the Crown's vicar in acquiring territory. The company directorate in London would be in broad control. In a particular area of operations a company officer called administrator would exercise executive power. The Colonial Office in London would keep remote watch to protect justice and to restrain rapacity, with general regard for indigenous peoples' welfare. The Crown's high commissioners nearer to the field of operations would keep track of activities and would have power of veto on appointment of administrators and on their exercise of ordinance-making authority. Elaborations and alterations of arrangements in face of unfolding opportunities and requirements would be subject to the Crown's approval by order-in-council.

The company's role and measure of its accomplishments were not uniform over all areas within its span of activity. The circumstances differentiating its achievements in one place from another related to distances, accesses, the nature of terrain, diversity of resources, climate, the tsetse fly as a factor affecting use of animal-drawn transport, and varying success in obtaining concessions from native rulers.

North of the Zambesi River and thence eastward to the region of Lake Nyasa, its mandate in settlement and governance was slight. There the tasks of governmental administration connected with company enterprises were largely handled by functionaries of the Crown in London, and such institutions as were developed reflected the British mode. South of the Zambesi white settlers entered in appreciable numbers and there the company operated as a governing apparatus; institutions there took their forms from the Dutch-Roman legal system applied in the Cape.

At the outset of the venture, the California-sized expanse between the Limpopo and the Zambesi was shown on maps as Matabeleland and Mashonaland. The names were derived from indigenous groups. The Matabele had entered a generation earlier, after the Boers had routed them from the Transvaal, where they had come in consequence of an extrusion from Natal incidental to slaughterous tribal warfare marking the emergence of the Zulu nation. Like the Zulu, of whom they were an offshoot, the Matabele were a warrior people, with a hierarchy corresponding to an order-of-battle. The term "Mashona" was an invidious collective noun applied by the Matabele to a hodgepodge of tribal remnants left in the wake of other and earlier invasions stemming from the convulsions in Natal. Existing precariously and supinely, the Mashona served as target for intermittent raids in which the Matabele tested their military skill, took capitives, and aggrandized their herds. Accordingly, the Mashona, though more numerous, were accounted tributaries of the Matabele. The original concession taken over by the company pertained to Mashonaland. The grantor was the Matabele king, Lobengula, personally a primitive hedonist and no devotee of war.

Differences over terms of the concession gave rise to disputes. These became acute when the company blocked Matabele raids against the Mashona. Lobengula rued the concession and tried to rescind it. The company resisted. The Matabele rose. Despite huge superiority in numbers, they were outmatched by the white men's tactical versatility. They lost the war, a substantial portion of their arms, and their king, who died in flight. The upshot left the company in charge as virtual successor to Lobengula. Matabeleland and Mashonaland were subsumed under a new name honoring the founder. An order-in-council ratified the combination.

Violence soon erupted again. A miscellany of grievances rankled the Matabele, acute among them a sense of having been cheated in the distribution of the late Lobengula's herds. The Matabele rose at an opportunity resulting from an illicit diversion of a large portion of the company's forces for an ill-conceived and bungled sortie, known to history as the Jameson Raid, designed to spark an overthrow of government in the Transvaal. Much to the dismay of white settlers' naïve expectations of collective gratitude, the Mashona pitched in on their old tormentors' side. The settlers barely held on. After seven highly dangerous months the rebellion was quelled. Indigenous militancy was daunted by defeat. Tribal forces were disarmed once and for all. The whites' presence was now premised on conquest. They were conscious of the land as one they had fought for rather than one they were in by sufferance. Thus they early took on identity as Rhodesians, even while emphasizing, as in our own time, Britishness in sentimental and ceremonial matters.

Philip Mason's *The Birth of a Dilemma* portrays the ensuing situation in which "two races, masters and conquered, ... poles apart, not only in tool-making techniques and in social organization, but in what they expected life to bring them, in their attitudes toward leisure, work and money" faced each other across a separating gulf which neither expected would be bridged within a calculable future. Though juxtaposed, they were mutually alien. What would appeal to one group as normal would be outrageous to the other. Development clashed with traditionalism, the needs of industry with habits of subsistence and barter. In such situations, recurrent in history, the texture of life can be rough and justice problematic. Moreover, an appraisal of the whites by the high commissioner, on a visit from the Cape late in 1897, found the "number of competent men available ... small, and the amount of riffraff ... considerable." Yet, onward after the rebellion, Southern Rhodesia would become, by general account, one of the world's notably tranquil and secure lands.

While distributing no dividends, the company, in the assured tone of a forthrightly imperial age, periodically informed stockholders of good works done or progressing in suppressing slave traffic, eradicating pestilence, taming wilderness, developing transport, and stimulating production. Thanks to having misused its command of forces and to the resulting opportunity for rebellion, the company system lost some of its credit with the Crown and, eventually, with the settlers. It had to yield a measure of its authority in accepting the presence of a resident representative of the high commissioner in the Cape and in vacating to him its control of local forces. Identity between company and settlers weakened. The latter tendency would increase after Rhodes's death in 1902.

As both cause and effect of this divergence, elements of representation were introduced into the internal structure stage by stage, with the Crown's approval. Apparently from the beginning, Southern Rhodesian politics reflected great preoccupation with personal qualities of leadership—a still persistent trait. An appointive council, instituted in 1895, was supplemented in 1898 by provision for a legislative council consisting of five appointed and four popularly elected members. In 1903 the appointed and elected portions were equalized. In 1911 the elected portion became a majority. In 1913 the elected majority was raised to two-thirds in a council of eighteen. The underlying electorate reflected Rhodes's precept of "equal rights for all civilized men, irrespective of races, south of the Zambesi." Qualifications were conceived according to white men's standards and expressed as minimums in income and cash value of property, but with no ethnic differentiations stipulated. For the moment and for a long future, a preponderantly white electorate was assured. At some point in progress the prevailing complexion might shift, but it would be feasible to raise requirements and thus to slow a trend toward an indigenous majority.

Southern Rhodesia had not yet become self-sustaining when the original charter lapsed. The Crown was averse to assume the company's operating deficits. Incorporation into the self-governing Union of South Africa, formed in 1910 from the erstwhile

British colonies in the Cape and Natal and the two former Boer republics in the Transvaal and the Orange Free State, subdued and annexed by the Crown in 1903, was an alternative possibility, but it found scant favor among the settlers. Their elected councillors opted for a ten-year extension of the charter and company rule, with a proviso for complete self-government if and when it should become economically practicable in the interim. Parliament enacted these terms.

Decision on the question of Southern Rhodesia's post-charter status was prompted by adjudication, in the Judicial Committee of the Privy Council in Britain, of a legal issue involving ownership of unalienated lands there. Claims were argued on behalf of the native tribes, the company, the settlers, and the Crown, with the verdict going for the Crown. That outcome removed all incentive for the company to spend on further improvements. Company rule thereby lost all appeal for the settlers.

Three possibilities were now open for Southern Rhodesia. It might become a Crown colony under British tutelage, join the Union of South Africa as a province, or have autonomous government in association with the Crown. The first found no favor. The issue crystallized as between the second and third paths. Despite the British and the South African governments' preferences for amalgamation with the Union, a referendum, with about 15,000 voting, resulted in a 3:2 ratio for autonomy. Arrangements were worked out between Southern Rhodesia's elected leaders and the British government. There was no question of imposing terms, for the British government did not administer the place, finance it, or have forces there, and its relationship to the country was not prescriptive.

Company rule was dissolved, and the company freed to pursue its primary goal, profits. Formalities of annexation to the Crown were performed—a paradox, in view of the judicial ruling retroactively vesting in the Crown title to Southern Rhodesia's residual lands. After a brief interval for elections and organization, authority to govern in Southern Rhodesia, along with title to residual lands, was devolved upon an establishment formed in pursuance of an act of the British Parliament, referred to as the constitution of 1923 and subject to amendment only by the same Parliament. This act placed formal executive functions in a Crown-appointed governor. He would act on advice of ministers of the locality except with regard to granting or withholding assent to legislation, on matters other than firearms and liquor, discriminatory against the indigenous population. Veto rights as to such legislation were reserved to the government in London. Operational executive power was placed in a seven-member cabinet, chosen from and made accountable to a legislative chamber of thirty members elected from fifteen two-member districts, at intervals no longer than five years, by voters qualifying by nationality, age, and annual income (initially set by statute at 200 pounds), and without regard to race. A second legislative chamber, though authorized, was never created. Only one item of public policy—regulation of mining royalties—was reserved from the legislature's competence.

The two other areas within the company's span of activities also were shortly given new standing, but not on a parity with Southern Rhodesia, for their histories and circumstances were different in that they had not been subject to conquest, their white settlers were relatively few, and development of representative institutions and local administration had lagged. Neither of them would be formally annexed to the Crown or provided with institutions of self-government. Northern Rhodesia became a Crown colony, Nyasaland was called a protectorate, and both were placed under the Crown's administrative tutelage with only rudimentary local representative institutions. In Northern Rhodesia institutions grew stage by stage, roughly paralleling those in Southern Rhodesia in charter times, but Nyasaland did not, for three decades, progress beyond appointive representation.

Southern Rhodesia's then newly achieved status, more pertinent to this account, deserves elaboration. It was that of a self-governing colony—a phrase implicit of contradiction, because colonies are by definition supposed to be not self-governing, but a phrase enshrined, nevertheless, in British constitutional usage. Canada and New Zealand had achieved that status in the mid-nineteenth century, and Australia had done so a little later. At the outset of their periods as self-governing colonies, the British government yielded control over their internal affairs except for a veto power over legislation affecting selective items reserved to the Crown in London —such as land policy, immigration, control of military forces, and constitutional amendments—while in external matters their affairs were completely in British hands. Thereupon, their Crown-appointed governors were reduced to ceremonial functions. The official channels between London and the so-

called self-governing colonies were no longer directive or executive but became mutual in the manner
of diplomatic interchange. Late in the nineteenth
century, the self-governing colonies were granted a
role in commercial negotiations with other governments. In 1905 they achieved complete autonomy in
commercial treaty relations. In 1907 reservations to
the Crown in London of certain aspects of legislative authority were largely abandoned, and the self-
governing colonies were restyled as self-governing
Dominions. In 1910 the Union of South Africa, and
in 1922 the Irish Free State, acceded to similar
status. All these Dominions entered the state system
in their own right as members of the League of
Nations. In the early nineteen-twenties, however,
they had not yet begun to avail themselves of the
opportunity for exchanging diplomatic representa-
tives with governments outside the British system.

Thus, in choosing the status of a self-governing
colony, the Southern Rhodesian electorate followed
a well-established mode with a fairly well defined
course of development in prospect. The status was
self-governing rather than colonial. Onward from
the constitution of 1923 the British government's
relations with Southern Rhodesia were handled not
through the Colonial Office but through the Dominions Office. The ties were quasidiplomatic in character rather than directive or executive—a distinction
of basic significance. Each government was represented for substantive purpose by a high commissioner. As a corollary, the new office of governor in
Southern Rhodesia was merely formal and honorific
—a personification of constitutional monarchy. The
occupant was appointed by London, with Southern
Rhodesia's concurrence. Nominally, he was com-

mander in chief of Southern Rhodesia's forces, while operative direction rested with authorities of the locality. As in the past, Southern Rhodesia's budget was in no part a charge upon the British exchequer, and its public service was entirely independent of the British government regarding appointment, promotion, discipline, and every other aspect. The restricted veto power, reserved to the government in London, was never used.

Theoretically speaking, Parliament in London could repeal its enactment of Rhodesia's constitution and substitute for it some other design drawn at its own discretion. Again theoretically, it retained power to legislate in the same fields in which it had conveyed legislative authority to the Southern Rhodesian legislature. In practice, such matters were governed by a convention, in the sense of an agreed usage, barring British initiative in interposing in Southern Rhodesia's affairs. A facet of this convention was that the British Parliament would undertake to amend or to repeal any portion of the constitution only at the request of the Southern Rhodesian government. No statute or treaty specified these inhibitory principles, but their existence was acknowledged by ministers of the Crown.

Southern Rhodesia issued its own passports, had control of its own foreign commerce, could and did establish consulates of its own abroad, and, in its standing under the 1923 constitution, in 1948 became a founding member of the General Agreements on Tariffs and Trade. Yet it was not fully and formally in the state system. Unlike the Dominions, it did not have a franchise in the League of Nations. Unlike the Dominions, it would not become a member of the United Nations. Respecting governments outside the Commonwealth, Southern Rhodesia's diplomatic representation was handled through British channels, usually by Southern Rhodesian officers assimilated into the British diplomatic establishment.

In 1926, the United Kingdom and the Dominions were declared to be "equal in status, in no way subordinate one to another in any aspect of their domestic or external affairs, though united by a common allegiance to the Crown, and freely associated as members of the British Commonwealth of Nations." Thereafter the Dominions Office in London was known as the Office of Commonwealth Relations, and as such it continued to handle affairs with Southern Rhodesia. In 1931, all last forms of reserved legislative power over the Dominions were vacated by the British Parliament under the Statute of Westminster. This formal change did not apply to Southern Rhodesia. From 1933 onward, however, Southern Rhodesia's chief of government was legally titled prime minister—a style reserved for independencies in British usage. In stately pronouncements Southern Rhodesia was customarily listed along with the Dominions. Moreover, and more importantly, after 1933 the Southern Rhodesian prime minister participated in Commonwealth affairs on a parity, in most aspects, with Dominion prime ministers. On the eve of World War II, by general account, Dominion status, and with it an acknowledged station in the state system, was an early and short step away for Southern Rhodesia, though, to be sure, no contract to that effect had been made.

Subsequent events briefly took another turn, toward combination of the two Rhodesias and Nyasaland in a collaborative arrangement called a federation. The idea of such a combination had a history.

In 1923 a policy statement issued as a White Paper by the British government stated, with respect to Kenya and in view of its inherent African character, a principle of paramountcy for indigenous interests over those of immigrants. Indians composed the immigrant group then in mind. White settlers in Kenya wondered, in some anxiety, whether the idea might not be applied against them as well, and white settlers elsewhere in British Africa wondered whether the principle might not be extended to their lands. They pressed for and, in 1927, elicited another White Paper affirming complementarity between indigenous and white progress and a rightful share in economic and political development for immigrant communities. In 1930 the British government revived and amplified the 1923 principle and extended it generally to colonies in East Africa. Such colonies were depicted as being held in trust for the indigenous peoples, and their white settlers' anxiety was stirred anew. One result was a prompting of Northern Rhodesian whites to take active interest in amalgamating with Southern Rhodesia, a land generally assumed to be too far along toward independence on the premises of its 1923 constitution to come within the scope of the policy enunciated.

It was not an entirely new idea. Fifteen years or so previously the chartered company had tentatively sponsored a merger of the two Rhodesias for the sake of economy. Throughout the nineteen-twenties Northern Rhodesia's whites, small in number, had recurringly discussed the advantages of diluting indigenous preponderance and throwing off Colonial Office domination by uniting with Southern Rhodesia. The idea had an economic appeal in view of their respective needs and resources. In the late nineteen-twenties the British government, adding Nyasaland to the pattern, referred the question to a royal commission for study. Its report, taking account of indigenous opposition north of the Zambesi, opposed amalgamation for the near future but accepted it in principle and recommended, for the interim, closer coordination through an interterritorial consultative council to consist of Southern Rhodesia's prime minister and the other two areas' respective royal governors.

World War II, which interposed before any step could be taken, itself necessitated closer administrative collaboration by greatly stimulating industrial activity. An interterritorial secretariat was set up by the two Rhodesias and then embellished along lines earlier recommended by the royal commission. In effect the arrangement provided an avenue for applying administrative energy and talents from Southern Rhodesia on problems to the north. Short-term successes, plus concern for joint development of the Zambesi's hydroelectric potential, again stimulated designs for amalgamating the Rhodesias. These elicited a British proposal of a federal formula as a less drastic alternative. A proviso for including Nyasaland was added. On these bases, the British government gave strong support, and in 1953 Parliament enacted a constitution for a so-called federation, subject to ratification by referendum in Southern Rhodesia and by vote of the legislative council in the other two colonies. The plan took effect by order-in-council in October of 1953. A ten year initial limitation and a provision for a constitutional review after seven years placed its future in question from the start.

The federation's intricacies are of small material

relevance here. Federal concerns were enumerated as defense, banking, commerce, tariffs, currency, company regulation, immigration, naturalization, transport, communications, railways, aviation, posts, telegraph, telephones, higher education for all groups, and basic education for all groups except the indigenous sector. Local government, police, native affairs (including native education), agriculture, health, and labor and trade unions remained within territorial jurisdiction. The power of the purse was mostly federalized. A legislature of thirty-six was provided—eighteen from Southern Rhodesia, eleven from Northern Rhodesia, and seven from Nyasaland. Two elected indigenous members and one nominated white member from each of the three territories represented indigenous interests. A weighted standing committee of the legislature had veto power, subject to being overruled by the governor general or by Parliament in London, over legislation considered discriminatory against the indigenous peoples. Formal executive power was vested in the governor general, appointed by the Crown. Operational executive power rested with a cabinet responsible to the legislature.

The federal constitution was superimposed on existing governmental arrangements. The United Kingdom was the ruling element in Northern Rhodesia and Nyasaland, while Southern Rhodesia remained self-governing. This jerrybuilt affair—to call it a federation is a misnomer—had the instability inherent in a stool with disparate legs. The wonder is not that it did not last beyond its ten years, but that it held up at all. Was there ever a chance of its becoming an independent federal dominion? That possibility, with its corollary of permanent Southern

Rhodesian dominance, damned the undertaking in the view of indigenous nationalist groups in the other two territories. The need of a more assured status was urged by successive federation prime ministers. The British government agreed, but its royal commission, set up to conduct the scheduled constitutional review, recommended rights of secession for component territories at the end of the prescribed ten years. Federation leaders saw in this a violation of the British prime minister's advance assurances concerning the commission's terms of reference. Defenders of British policy countered that the prime minister's assurances had been vague and equivocal rather than explicitly and intentionally deceptive.

The royal commission's action was less a death sentence than a burial certificate, and British policy was probably perplexed rather than intentionally devious. The federation had produced many results, among them the unintended effect of stimulating indigenous nationalist movements, especially in the components north of the Zambesi, where tensions and turbulence increased. In 1959 indigenous nationalist violence, directed less at the specifics of federation than at white ascendancy in general, interrupted Southern Rhodesia's civil tranquility, which had persisted since 1897. To Great Britain, maintenance of the federation became a less and less attractive prospect. The collapse of the 1956 Suez campaign, added to the exactions of the recent world war, made manifest a severe reduction of Britain's capacity for the management of empire. Three years after the Suez debacle the British prime minister was repeating across Africa, as a phrase of acquiescence and abdication, a metaphor from Thomas a Kempis about winds of change. A subordinate minister gave point to the expression, two years later, in explaining Britain's reluctance to uphold order in the federal components where order was Britain's responsibility. Britain, he said, had lost the will to govern there.

Britain's inconstancy toward federation still rankles among whites in Rhodesia—the land's name since the federal dissolution at the close of 1963 and the emergence into independence of Northern Rhodesia as Zambia and Nyasaland as Malawi. In their view, Britain's false assurances of support for federation misled Rhodesia and cheated it of Dominion status at a time when it was well within reach. So harsh a judgment is probably not warranted, for, in turning reluctant about the federation's future, the British government was coming to terms with the reality of its own weakness rather than being purposely fickle.

Initiative for a new constitution was taken on Southern Rhodesia's behalf in 1960, at a time when the end of federation was in prospect, though Britain had not yet explicitly said so and the more ardent supporters of federation were still loath to acknowledge the portents. The process of producing a new constitution began with preparatory interchanges between the two governments. A constitutional convention in Southern Rhodesia followed, with Britain's Minister for Commonwealth Relations presiding and with all politically significant segments of the population, including indigenous nationalist groups, represented. A White Paper containing the convention's recommendations and a summary in layman's language of proposed constitutional changes was published and circulated among the electorate. Thereafter a referendum was held.

The British Parliament then enacted terms for the new constitution. An order-in-council was issued to prescribe steps for effecting it, including enactment by the Southern Rhodesian legislature of interim changes in existing election laws to conform to the prospective constitution. These steps were completed in November, 1962. Elections were held a month later; the new constitution took full effect.

The new constitution provided for two voter rolls respectively with higher and lower qualifications measured in combined factors of income, property, and education. It provided for two correlated sets of overlapping single-member electoral districts—fifty in one set and fifteen in the other, for a legislative chamber totaling sixty-five members. Each higher-qualified voter would get a full-value vote in one of the fifty districts and a quarter-value vote in an overlapping district from among the fifteen. A lower-qualified voter would get a full-value vote in one of the fifteen districts and a quarter-vote in an overlapping district from among the fifty. The aim thus was to increase the number of indigenous voters by liberalizing the standards, at the same time to moderate the impact, and, by intermixing constituencies, to discourage racial extremism among candidates. Besides a bill of rights, the constitution established a multiracial constitutional council empowered to compel reconsideration of any legislation found at variance with the bill of rights. The new constitution gave Rhodesia power to amend the constitution thenceforth, with certain exceptions. Some parts of the constitution could be amended by a two-thirds majority of the legislature, but most provisions, including the most important, were made subject to amendment only by a process including, besides the requisite legislative majority, either approval by concurrent majorities of all racial groups voting separately in a referendum or assent by the British sovereign—meaning in practice the government in London. Such portions were called entrenched clauses. In addition, certain provisions were made subject to amendment only by the sovereign through order-in-council—meaning by the British government. Besides extending the sanctity of mining royalties, the relevant provision pertained to the governor's office and its functions, including assent to legislation.

A main circumstance prompting the move for constitutional revision was a tendency, as seen by Southern Rhodesians, for the British government to interpose, at least implicitly, more and more in the country's internal affairs, a tendency probably inherent in federal arrangements between two British-administered colonies and self-governed Southern Rhodesia. According to Southern Rhodesia's sense of the situation, influences working on the British government would press ever more strongly toward establishing indigenous ascendency as a precondition to independence, in place of existing franchise qualifications which, though nonracial in principle, for all practical purposes made white ascendency certain for an indefinite future and sought furthermore to ensure maintenance of standards reflecting the ruling group's values as criteria under which an eventual indigenous majority would be generated. A companion purpose was to rid the 1923 constitution of reserved clauses subjecting the Southern Rhodesian legislature's authority respecting indigenous affairs to a power of veto to be exercised at the British government's discretion. Obviously, the general aim was to round out local autonomy.

The British White Paper issued in preparation for the referendum gave promise of an end to reserved clauses. This was taken by the electorate to mean more than it did. The constitution was envisioned as a penultimate step to Dominion standing. Technically, the relevant promise was fulfilled. The reality, however, after Southern Rhodesians examined what Parliament had enacted, disappointed their expectations. Southern Rhodesia's dominant group conjured up fears lest the British government, unrestrained by any convention, should tamper unilaterally with constitutional clauses subject to change by order-in-council. The prize of Dominion status seemed as elusive as ever. Bitterness and chagrin, justified or not, rose with the approach of election time. Indigenous nationalist groups, after having signified support for the new constitution at earlier stages, reversed themselves, denounced the constitution, boycotted the election, and undertook to sabotage it by terrorist activities. By a modest margin in popular votes, the election produced a large legislative majority for a political grouping, the Rhodesia Front, determined on independence on its own terms, with or without British consent.

In a somewhat ambiguous course, the British government also undertook to alter relationships in an opposite direction, but it took a while for the antithesis of purpose to emerge into clarity. A few months after the advent of the new constitution, Britain's appropriate minister disclosed to the House of Commons an intention to make Rhodesian independence a subject for the whole Commonwealth's consideration and concurrence. The Commonwealth, whose continued existence the British government prized as a memento of former power and scope, now consisted largely of new independencies suddenly translated from explicit subordination to titular statehood. Rhodesia had long antedated most of them in practical self-government. Now they had preceded Rhodesia into formal independence. For them as for older Commonwealth members, independence terms had been worked out with Great Britain only, not made the business of a collectivity of governments. Theretofore, the Commonwealth membership had no hand in determining Rhodesia's constitutional status. In the view of Rhodesia's new regime, Britain's new attitude amounted to an unprecedented unilateral alteration of conditions affecting Rhodesia's future. As a mollifying gesture, the British government dropped the anomolous word "colony" from Rhodesia's official designation and reavowed the convention against British initiatives affecting Rhodesia's standing, subject to a proviso against regressive steps regarding the indigenous population. Conditions for a stalemate were thus defined. Intermittent discussions of a way out made small headway on particulars. A shift in party leadership, bringing in a new prime minister, signaled a stiffening on Rhodesia's part in the spring of 1964, but by early autumn he indicated abandonment of any plan to assume independence unilaterally. Then, following a shift of party control in the British election of that autumn, the issue heightened again. The British government moved more unequivocally in the direction of applying to Southern Rhodesia an equivalent of the 1930 pronouncement regarding indigenous paramountcy in place of the precept in effect since 1923.

Paradoxically, the undertaking called for drastic intensification of authority over a distant land and people after will, and indeed capacity, to govern abroad had ebbed. Britain, which had been promoting dependencies into self-government wholesale, undertook a purpose entailing subordination of a polity long experienced in autonomy—and did so without command of means to give purpose to that effect. How the British government was prompted to its course, and how it has fared, brings into the account the United Nations' role—a topic dealt with in the next section.

As a closing point, an observer of international affairs is likely to be reminded often of the capriciousness with which expressions of moral approbation or censure are applied in discussions of great affairs. He should not necessarily dismiss their worth and relevance, but he should take heed how such ideas tend to pass in and out of fashion and, much as a man views ladies' hats, regard them with detached interest while being intent primarily on what lies beneath.

Over recent generations, shifts in moral tone have marked Britain's approach to questions of empire. When Britain was encouraging settlement on new frontiers, settlers were usually portrayed as agents of civility, tranquility, and development. Later, with empire running its course, settlers became objects of disdain, and tranquility came to be thought of as oppression, civility as coercive imposition of white men's preferences, and development as exploitation. Values involved in issues of central control versus

local autonomy were inverted from one stage to another. In an earlier time the British government's
attempts to dominate settlers' affairs in far places
were generally regarded as imperial manifestations,
and Britons of libertarian outlook lined up on the
settlers' side—as in the instance of the American
Revolution. Subsequently, with a shift of emphasis
to decolonization, labels were reversed. Settlers were
tagged as imperialist. London's assertions of authority took over libertarian watchwords. Thus it has
been with Rhodesia.

The white Rhodesians' public standing with the
British has shifted. Once they were Britain's favorite
colonials. The founder's reputation had rubbed off
on them. Their manpower contributions in two
world wars, notably large among all the overseas
realms, were remembered. Statesmen and writing
men gave them good marks as solid people of sound
outlook. Within a brief span, with empire becoming
regarded as an encumbrance rather than an asset,
the prevailing tone changed, and Rhodesia's reputation sagged. The purpose in recounting this is not to
judge between contrasting views but to stress that in
such matters memory is short and reputation per-
ishable.

Inevitably, in such a circumstance, London's attitude became insouciant. A one-time federation prime
minister, Sir Roy Welensky, himself no apologist
for unilateral independence, has recalled to Laurens
van der Post: ". . . it is inconceivable how the Conservative Government treated us, how they kept on
changing their Secretaries of State before they had
a chance of getting to know us or our problems. One
of the last Ministers they sent out listened to me for
two hours with such obvious boredom that I gave up

in despair." Writing in *The New Yorker,* Calvin Trillin recounts a British high bureaucrat's description of Rhodesians as "really . . . an awfully second-rate people" and reports a view prevailing among British hierarchs "that not three of the Ministers in the Rhodesia Front Cabinet could be assistant postmasters in England." "They call themselves Ministers," he quotes a British diplomat. "But they're nothing more than town councillors, really." Correct or not, such estimates afford a risky premise for policy in an adversary situation.

III. REBELLION AND RETRIBUTION

It is of the utmost importance that the United Nations should not be used as a dumping ground for hard decisions which are unpopular at home. For surely the U.N. is in no sense a world government which can step in where the national governments fear to tread.—Walter Lippmann

The 1964 British elections—bringing the Labour Party into authority in succession to the Conservatives, who had been in charge of policy during the life and death of the federation—marked a turn in the British government's approach to its impasse with Rhodesia.

The change had roots in contrasting traditional attitudes toward empire. Even in the heyday, embarrassment mingled with pride in British thoughts regarding overseas extensions of authority. In a general way, Conservatives are successors to those who had affirmative attitudes about empire. Labourites are heirs to opposed values. By the nineteen-sixties, with Britain's one-time huge scope reduced to a recollection, neither major party could be properly described as a devotee of empire, but a distinction has still persisted. Conservative attitudes toward retraction have varied from velleity to regret. Labourite attitudes have varied between inclination and enthusiasm. It is a difference between being liquidators of empire from necessity and liquidators of empire by conviction and ideology.

The White Paper of 1927, referred to above as affirming complementarity in development between settlers and the indigenous population, was issued under Conservative auspices. The contrasting declaration of 1930 on behalf of indigenous paramountcy was a Labour product. Conservatives in power had encouraged federation. Labour out of power opposed it. The 1961 constitution for Rhodesia was delivered by Conservatives ascendant in London. The Labour Party, then in minority, had opposed it and urged in its place an entirely new formula which would have displaced the existing structure with indigenous dominance. It did so without detailing means for accomplishing the end being urged, a prerogative of parties out of power.

The two parties have proved much alike in wishing to find a way of making conditions for Rhodesia's formal independence agreeable to the Commonwealth as a whole, meaning particularly the proliferating novices to statehood among the membership. The problem of how to do that in a way acceptable to those in authority in Rhodesia on a basis legitimate under British law has stumped Britain's successive ruling parties. Both have had to face up to a hard fact—namely, the gap between Britain's wish to exert authority and its command of means. The basic difference in approaches has related to the parties' respective attitudes toward United Nations attempts to interpose. It is in point therefore to consider a succession of relevant activities in the United Nations realm, beginning with positions on the future of non-self-governing territories in general.

What the United Nations Charter itself says on that subject is a reflection of a reference to "the rights of all people to choose the form of government under which they will live" included by President Roosevelt and Prime Minister Churchill in the

Atlantic Charter of 1941 among the "certain common principles . . . on which they base their hopes for a better future for the world." The language originated with Churchill, who apparently regarded the thought as a fillip in public relations rather than a proposition in policy, for he later disavowed any intention of forwarding the liquidation of empire. In any event, the thought would find expression in Chapter XI of the United Nations Charter, pertaining to non-self-governing territories. One of the articles articulates "the principle that the interests of the inhabitants of those territories are paramount." Its terms impose "as a sacred trust the obligation to promote to the utmost, within the system of international peace and security established by the present Charter, the well-being of the inhabitants." The obligation is elaborated to embrace political, economic, social, and educational advancement, just treatment and protection against abuses, development of self-government and free political institutions with due account of inhabitants' political aspirations, furtherance of international peace and security, and promotion of constructive measures along social, economic, and scientific lines. Members responsible for administering such territories are obligated to make regular reports to the United Nations including statistical and other technical information regarding economic, social, and educational conditions.

In 1953 the General Assembly undertook to state at length appropriate standards for guiding subordinate territories into self-government and for determining their achievement of it. The vote was 32 to 19, with 6 abstentions, and the resolution passed by virtue of a previous 30 to 26 vote holding the matter in view not to be a matter of importance and thus not to require a two-thirds majority. Such obviously relevant criteria as military, administrative, legislative, and judicial autonomy were included. In addition the resolution listed, in wide variety, points of civil virtue and institutional and personal freedom, including such items as a free and secret ballot, protected personal rights to criticize government, the existence of more than one political party, and equality of right among all adults relevant to determining the form of government. As aptly observed at the time, a large portion of the governments voting in the affirmative could not have qualified. The same still holds with respect to a large portion of the much expanded General Assembly.

The next relevant General Assembly resolution, coming in 1960, would fit Raymond Aron's depiction of self-determination as the political absolute of our time. Referring to non-self-governing territories as an aggregate, the resolution called for "immediate transfer of all powers to those territories without any conditions and reservations, in accordance with their freely expressed will and desire, without any distinctions as to race, creed or color, in order to enable them to enjoy complete independence and freedom." The vote was 89 to 0, with 9 abstentions. A year later, the Assembly elaborated the concept with a resolution "emphasizing that inadequacy of political, economic, social and educational preparedness should never serve as a pretext for delaying independence." By the same resolution a special committee participated in by seventeen governments was established to report a year later on how to give effect to the idea. The vote was 97 to 0, with 4 abstaining.

37

Southern Rhodesia's status arose as an issue before the Assembly soon thereafter. It was at a time shortly following the issuance in London of the order-in-council proclaiming the 1961 constitution and detailing procedures for bringing it into effect. Southern Rhodesia's numerically marginal indigenous nationalists had shifted from acquiescence to hostility toward the new constitution and were resorting to sabotage and violence in hope of somehow forcing British interposition and overturning the government. The Assembly's Fourth Committee, taking note of the circumstance that the United Kingdom had never registered Southern Rhodesia as a non-self-governing territory within the purview of Chapter XI of the Charter or filed a report as called for under its provisions, prompted an Assembly resolution asking the new special committee to consider and report whether Southern Rhodesia was indeed self-governing. The Assembly passed such a resolution in early 1962 by a vote of 57 to 21, with 24 abstaining. Following the committee's report, the General Assembly passed a resolution in June, 1962, affirming Southern Rhodesia to be a non-self-governing territory in the sense of Chapter XI of the Charter. The vote was 73 to 1, with 27 abstentions. As an added thought—accepted by a vote of 75 to 1, with 23 abstentions—the resolution called on Great Britain to summon a new constitutional conference and to bring about a new constitution on the immediate basis of one man-one vote.

In the following October the General Assembly issued two more resolutions on how the United Kingdom should handle Rhodesian matters. The first, passed by an 83 to 2 vote with 11 abstentions, called on the United Kingdom to effect release of

African nationalist leaders and activitists under duress. The second, passed by an 81 to 2 vote with 19 abstentions, besides repeating the earlier call for a new constitutional convention and one man-one vote, urgently called on the United Kingdom to withhold the constitution of 1961 from going into effect and to cancel scheduled elections. It also called on the Secretary General to lend good offices to bring about the aims.

A year later, 1963, the Security Council for the first time took note of the Rhodesian situation in considering a proposed action calling on the United Kingdom not to transfer any power or attribute of sovereignty to Rhodesia incidentally to dissolution of the federation and, in the same connection, not to permit reversion of any armed forces or aircraft. The proposal failed because of a negative vote by the United Kingdom itself. Subsequently in that autumn the General Assembly dealt with Rhodesia in two more resolutions. One, passed by a 90 to 2 vote with 13 abstentions, echoed the Security Council proposal vetoed by the United Kingdom. The second, passed by a 73 to 2 vote with 19 abstentions, declared the situation in Rhodesia to constitute a threat to the peace, urged the United Kingdom to withhold independence from Rhodesia pending establishment of majority rule, and again urged a new constitutional conference.

Such was the United Nations' record up to the time of the watershed election in Britain. During the Conservatives' tenure, the British government responded consistently to these initiatives. In the background was that government's view expressed during the General Assembly's consideration in 1952 of the cited resolution regarding standards for judging self-government. At that time the British government challenged the General Assembly's competence in the matter—not simply its practical competence but its legal competence in view of the limitations of the General Assembly's role under the Charter to such functions as discussing, considering, making recommendations, and calling attention. The British government abstained from voting, as it did again on the 1960 and 1961 resolutions calling for immediate, unconditional, wholesale independence.

Through successive stages of the 1962 proceedings in which the General Assembly sought to countermand British law in regard to Southern Rhodesia's status, the British government adhered to an unequivocal position. To an adamant majority during the Fourth Committee's preparatory deliberations, a British spokesman unavailingly explained Southern Rhodesia's constitutional background and standing in details similar to those included here in the preceding chapter. A short time later Britain's prime minister of the time and key cabinet colleagues in London went over the same ground with a delegation from the special committee on decolonization. Before the General Assembly as a whole, Britain's spokesman disputed the body's warrant to interfere, decried mere assertion of such right as a vindication of it, and emphasized Britain's lack of access to such data regarding Southern Rhodesia as would enable it to comply with reporting requirements under Chapter XI of the Charter. On repeated subsequent occasions before the General Assembly and its committees, British spokesmen explained Britain's lack of legal and operative powers to take the actions being demanded. Before the Security Council in 1963 Britain explained in detail Southern Rhodesia's self-governing character and challenged the propriety of United Nations interposition in view of the ban in paragraph 7 of Article 2 of the Charter against intervention in matters essentially within a state's domestic jurisdiction. Throughout the British position was as once stated in the General Assembly's Fourth Committee: "No resolution . . . of this Committee or of the Security Council or of the General Assembly can make the status of Southern Rhodesia what it is not." On the proposition in 1962 of authorizing a study of Southern Rhodesia's status, Britain voted no. Thereupon it refused to participate even to the extent of registering abstentions from the General Assembly's successive votes.

The British arguments put into focus the practical purport of the successive General Assembly resolutions and the stillborn action in the Security Council. It was not a case of other governments being oblivious or unbelieving. Probably none of them doubted the limits of Britain's actual authority. The detailed truth of Britain's contentions was scarcely disputed at the various stages. What the British government was being called on to do was not to exercise powers in its possession but to presume powers beyond its possession. Implicitly but no less clearly, it was being pressed to denounce and to destroy the legitimacy vested in the existing Southern Rhodesian government, to override its existence, and radically to transform relationships by subjugating Southern Rhodesia. Such action would entail application of powers never before exercised by Great Britain over Southern Rhodesia. The intent, clearly enough, was coercive. The successive resolutions were summonses to battle, and Britain was supposed to fight it. The United Nations would be cast as decision-maker, with Britain in the role of agency.

While in opposition, the Labour Party prefigured a shift in the British approach. Disapproval of the 1961 constitution was recalled. The party leader, Harold Wilson, declared "no constitution . . . defensible which fails to allow the people . . . to control their own destinies"—a strong gesture of agreement with the general propositions endorsed by the General Assembly. "We have bitterly attacked the Southern Rhodesia Constitution for that, and a Labour Government would therefore alter it—we've made that very, very plain," he added. Implicit here was an intention irrespective of the existing Southern Rhodesian government's consent, but no indication how to enforce such an undertaking. "But we would go further," Mr. Wilson went on. "When these questions are debated at the United Nations, you would not find us voting in a collection of now, to some extent, discredited imperial powers." The precise import of that last expression was somewhat obscure, because by then Britain was being found not voting at all on relevant issues, but the words seemed to convey an intention to align with the majority at the United Nations on policy toward Rhodesia. Still further, the leader described the Labour Party as "totally opposed to granting independence to Southern Rhodesia so long as the Government of that country remains under the control of the white minority."

Obviously, "totally opposed" is as opposed as it is possible to be. That was a strong pledge. Fulfilling it would be a big order. By inference, with Labour in authority, Great Britain would not feel bound by any convention to refrain from legislating for Rhodesia except at the latter's request. The government there, legitimate under British law, would have to renounce its legitimacy or else be overborne. Somehow it must be brought to acquiesce or be coerced, so as to enable the British government to alter the rules of the game as a precondition, and at the very moment, of bowing out of it. The Rhodesian regime must be convinced of having no choice. It must be made to regard the question to be not what terms it might prefer but only what Britain might grant. The regime must be persuaded to see dire impracticability in a course of asserting independence on its own—a possibility in which interest was rekindled in consequence of the Labour Party's accession to authority in London. In the event Rhodesia ventured the course anyway, it must be brought to heel, as the new British prime minister put it.

The question of means? The British approach amounted to attempting to impose conditions of governance. To impose such conditions entails conquest. Conquest entails force. Force, however, was ruled out. The point, tacit at first, was made explicit as the issue drew to a head during the ensuing year and after the Archbishop of Canterbury had publicly alleged general church support for warfare against a recalcitrant Rhodesia. Countervailing voices were raised, including the prime minister's, lest the apparition of war alienate support of the policy. The Archbishop spoke for a marginal few. Opinion polls subsequently showed the proportion of British adults willing to go to such length as about one in sixteen. So Britain, the prime minister made clear, would not make a literal fight of it. The approach was the reverse of that taken by France under President Charles de Gaulle toward the National Liberation

Front (FLN) in Algeria. The French fought the FLN over terms of independence while acknowledging the adversary's succession to authority, whereas Britain would not fight but would not acknowledge the Rhodesian regime as entitled to continue into independence.

The eschewal of force was sorely disappointing in some quarters, and proposals for vicarious war were raised when the General Assembly's Trusteeship Committee demanded in a 95 to 2 vote that Britain "take all steps necessary to put an end to rebellion" if it should occur. The press reported that, while the resolution did not mention force, members left no doubt that force was what they meant. Assembled heads of various African states meeting at Accra as members of the Organization of African Unity echoed more explicitly the same sentiment for violence. Later on, the demand was echoed in successive Commonwealth conferences, where Britain's prime minister would be urged to ignore lack of public support and factors of military incapability and to embrace war for sake of principle. "Blood must flow," Zambia's president insisted. An assortment of African states would, unsuccessfully, press a resolution in the Security Council to direct Britain to take the field in forthright attack.

Rather than becoming an agent of others' directives, the British government's idea was to turn to the Commonwealth and to the United Nations—especially the latter, thereby marking another shift from former policy—for means to give effect to Britain's purposes. With their aid, penalties for attempting unilateral independence would be ostracism and deprivation. Rhodesia would be denied standing.

It would suffer commercial discriminations. It would in effect be made a pariah. The prospect, conveyed unequivocally to the Rhodesian government and electorate, presumably would deter any move to assert independence on the Rhodesian government's own terms and compel the regime to submit the country to Britain's terms instead. If deterrence failed, the reality of being cut off would soon do in the Rhodesian regime, whereupon some contrite successor group would yield to Britain's prescription. Rhodesia "cannot hope to defy Britain, the whole of the Commonwealth, nearly the whole of Africa, and the United Nations," the British prime minister said.

An aspect of the approach now taken by Britain was that of clarifying and sharpening issues with Rhodesia, something not accomplished during the Conservatives' tenure. It would be inaccurate to describe the British government as proceeding to define the conditions for Rhodesian independence. It never went that far toward contractual precision. It went only so far as to state "principles on which the British government would need to be satisfied before they were able to contemplate the grant of independence"—not conditions antecedent to action but conditions antecedent to consideration of the possibility. In the process of interchange, notwithstanding the prime minister's previous position, the British government relaxed insistence on rule by an indigenous majority as a precondition to independence. The conditions were distilled to five. Two of these related to guarantees reaching into the future—one to uphold progress toward majority rule in keeping with the principle enshrined in the 1961 constitution, the other to bar regressive amendment of the constitution. Two related to immediate matters—improvement in political status for the indigenous population and progress toward ending racial discrimination. The fifth related to proving acceptability "to the people of Rhodesia as a whole" as a basis for independence.

In months of recurrent negotiations attended by heightening tension, the last point proved the most critical and determinative as an issue. The British government, pressed within the Commonwealth and from the United Nations, was loath to accept approval registered through tribal hierarchies as authentically signifying consent by the generality of the indigenous peoples. The alternative would be to have an all-inclusive referendum. To the Rhodesian government such alternative seemed a certain shortcut to an electorate conceived on indigenous nationalist lines and at variance with Rhodesia's long established gradualist concept of qualifying voters. A three-member royal commission to consist of the Rhodesian chief justice and two others named by the respective governments was apparently agreed to as a device for formulating and applying a proper method for verifying indigenous attitudes on the question. Subsequently the British government affirmed both a requirement for making Britain's reluctance toward the 1961 constitution as a basis for independence known to those to be consulted in such a verification and Britain's freedom to disregard the outcome of such a test.

At that juncture the Rhodesian government attempted to cut the moorings. It had behind it the existing electorate's registered preference for the 1961 constitution as a basis for independence and also the circumstance that in interim elections held a year and a half previously, the Rhodesia Front,

known as leaning avowedly toward unilateral assertion of independence, had prevailed in all the fifty
legislative constituencies primarily for higher-qualified voters. In essence the rebellion consisted of pre-
suming, first, a power to amend the amending process
in the existing constitution with respect to the entrenched clauses by eliminating the requirement for
approval either by a referendum in which ethnic
groups would vote separately or alternately by the
Crown in London and submitting instead a requirement for additional approval by a two-thirds vote of
the legislature at a successive sitting; and, second, a
power to amend certain provisions reserved to the
Crown in London so as to provide a formal executive alternate to the Crown-appointed governor. In
form, the acts of presumption were on the part of
the Rhodesian legislature, thenceforth to be called
a Parliament. What the Rhodesians asserted was
constitutional autonomy on a Dominion-like basis.
Subsequently the regime would attempt to explain
the action as countenanced by terms of the 1961 constitution and therefore not an arrogation at all, but
the rationalization is farfetched and unconvincing.
Clearly the act was ultra vires of the constitution
whence the Rhodesian legislature and cabinet derived their existence. The term "rebellion" was and
is technically appropriate.

Great Britain's immediate response, taken on its
own authority, consisted, first, of a parliamentary
enactment declaring void the action taken by Rhodesia and authorizing actions by the Crown necessary to suppress the rebellion and, second, of a corollary order-in-council annulling the Rhodesian regime
and all its acts and subsuming all power over Rhodesia. Technically the two governments concerned

were now completely at loggerheads. The stake was authority to govern over Rhodesia. Each was claimant to such authority unconditionally. The positions were mutually exclusive. Theoretically and analytically, there was no longer a basis for negotiating. On paper, they seemed implicitly at war. In practice, of course, the Rhodesian regime remained in charge in Rhodesia, and the British government was making no move to challenge it on the premises.

Great Britain now turned to the United Nations as an instrumentality for dealing with Rhodesia. Up to that time, through 1965, Britain had persevered in insisting that Rhodesia was a self-governing country and its status no concern of the United Nations. In May it had abstained on a Security Council resolution, passed by a 7 to 0 vote, calling on Britain to act against unilateral independence and not to transfer sovereignty to Rhodesia. In October it had refused to voice a position on a General Assembly resolution, passed by 107 to 2, calling for steps to prevent or to end threatened rebellion in Rhodesia. On November 5, the General Assembly, by an 82 to 9 vote, with 18 abstentions, had resolved anew on the situation by recapitulating past positions, calling on Britain again to act as if in actual charge on the ground, and urging strong action in event of a unilateral move for independence. Great Britain declined to participate in voting. It declined again in the same forum immediately after Rhodesia's breakaway on a resolution, passed 102 to 2 with 1 abstention, calling on Britain to enforce all previous resolutions on Rhodesia and recommending Security Council action. In the Security Council next day, however, Britain joined in a resolution calling for withholding of recognition from the miscreant. Eight days later, Britain prompted a Security Council resolution in support of its own efforts against Rhodesia, most importantly by calling "upon all states to refrain from any action which would assist and encourage the illegal regime and, in particular, to desist from providing it with arms, equipment and military material, and to do their utmost in order to break all economic relations . . ., including an embargo on oil and petroleum products." The same resolution affirmed and applied to Rhodesia the General Assembly's 1960 resolution on unconditional independence for non-self-governing territories. By its vote in favor, Britain implicitly acknowledged a change in Rhodesia's status consistent with its new act of Parliament and order-in-council.

Thus Britain gave effect to its warnings designed to deter the event. It is interesting now to go back over the prime minister's dire predictions, coupled with his derision of Rhodesia's contrasting estimates of probable effects published as the break approached. Seemingly, the so-called town councillors and assistant postmasters were getting the shrewder economic advice. Statesmen are little given to acknowledging, let alone publicly analyzing, their mistakes. So the source of relevant British misestimates can only be guessed. The British government, it seems to me, could scarcely have placed such sanguine credence as it seemed to place in the efficacy of economic restrictions and political ostracism against a country able to meet so many of its own basic needs and accustomed to only marginal participation in formalities of what is called the state system. The power of such discriminatory measures, call them boycotts or sanctions, is a matter more of myth than experience. A fairly resourceful position and a measure of determination spell resiliency in face of such pressures, and notions of substituting them for applied military force are scarcely demonstrable. The American Civil War of a century ago, while not affording an analogy, would serve to illustrate a point. The South held up four years under a hugely effective interdiction of commerce, with the stringency of its situation steadily aggravated by continuous battle.

My press clippings for the fall and winter of 1965–66 abound with adumbrations of early counterrebellion in Rhodesia, most of them from unnamed British sources in London or at the United Nations. When, shortly following the resolution for sanctions, the British prime minister was assuring the Commonwealth of its being only a matter of weeks until Rhodesia's capitulation and when he was discussing details regarding a successor regime, he must surely have been counting on factors other than economic reduction. He may have anticipated an assertion of white Rhodesians' alleged latent Britishness. Perhaps he took heed of the stay-at-home factor, nearly 40 percent, in the Rhodesian referendum on independence, or was guided by the tone of Rhodesia's press, which was decidedly negative on the prospective unilateral move, or by a mood of reluctance shown by Rhodesian industrialists. He may have got unfounded advice from bureaucrats in the Office of Commonwealth Relations. Perhaps, in the vein of some British writers, Rhodesia's dominant group was written off as consisting of effete people, accustomed to being waited on and bound to wince at the first turn of the screw. All of these possibilities were suggested in British commentaries of the time. Whatever the premise, Great Britain counted, as Calvin Trillin has put it, on history's first political coup engineered by moderates.

As weeks lengthened into months, with small sign of coup or capitulation, problems of establishing a cogent system of commercial restrictions heightened. As one trouble, the bite indirectly affected Rhodesia's neighbors, including Zambia, Malawi, and Bechuanaland (now Botswana), in some respects more painfully than Rhodesia itself. The British, with some United States assistance, set up a special air lift to fill Zambia's needs for petroleum, an item singled out for special mention in the Security Council's relevant resolution as a possible key for bringing Rhodesia to a standstill. Some petroleum, though in reduced volume, continued to get through to Rhodesia via Mozambique. Premium prices paid in Rhodesia for gasoline above normal levels imposed in rationing probably enticed some of Zambia's airlifted supply. A new channel from South Africa was opened by purchases and gifts.

South Africa, itself a target of repeated proposals for punitive commercial restrictions in the United Nations, has been of a divided mind about Rhodesia's unilateral bid for independence. The tendency there was to regard the move as premature and imprudent but, once it had been made, to wish it success. For the South African government it was a question of opting between risks, that of being next in line if Rhodesia should be brought down and that of becoming embroiled through being an avenue for circumventing sanctions against Rhodesia. South Africa's announced policy was that of standing aloof, of doing nothing one way or the other to help or to hinder sanctions. The effect was to permit Rhodesia to acquire petroleum through South Africa, not theretofore a channel for such commerce. The British government pressed for closure of this access on grounds that South Africa was hindering sanctions by permitting abnormal trade. It became a question of defining what was normal. In declining, South Africa recited Britain's own arguments against United States importunities for curtailment of British trade with Cuba and North Vietnam.

An ostentatious challenge to the petroleum embargo was raised in early April when Greek tankers, chartered in a roundabout way, approached a Mozambique port with loads consigned, via pipeline, to a Rhodesian refinery. Delivery would have vitiated the whole idea of oil sanctions. Great Britain sought from the Security Council a warrant for using naval power to prevent such a happening. Under the Charter's terms, such a decision must be premised on the existence of an imminent threat to the peace. By a 10 to 0 vote with 5 abstentions, the Security Council passed a resolution alleging such threat to exist and authorizing action. Delivery was avoided. The pipeline continued to lie idle. Petroleum in modest sufficiency continued to reach Rhodesia.

By spring British policy was in a quandary. Britain was on record for a fight to the finish. It was also desirous of finishing the fight. At the United Nations and in the Commonwealth, and by its own laws as well, Britain was plighted to propositions that could be realized only by defeating Rhodesia, and that defeat did not appear to be forthcoming. Rhodesia also was desirous of an end to the impasse, on acceptable terms, of course, and what would be acceptable to Rhodesia would be hard to reconcile with what Britain was in position to vouchsafe. Cautious talks between emissaries about the possibility of talks between principals were scheduled. Both prime ministers faced outcries lest principles be deserted. Both prime ministers pledged intransigence on terms. It would be a quest of rapprochement between mutually exclusive positions. Discussions went on intermittently through spring and summer. At the annual Commonwealth conference, the British prime minister was placed on the defensive. The thought of Britain's parleying and temporizing with the Rhodesian adversary instead of pushing through to a violent ending drew imprecations, and there was talk of jeopardy to the Commonwealth's future. In response, the prime minister attached stiff conditions to further negotiations. It was Britain that would propose terms. They would be offered to Rhodesia as a last chance. A terminal date would be set—in sum, an ultimatum. After that, it would be a case of going back to the Security Council for a more drastic punitive formula.

The efforts to negotiate, now under an ultimatum, would eventuate into a face-to-face meeting of the respective prime ministers aboard a British warship. Did they meet as a prime minister of a sovereign state and a prime minister of a polity of subordinate station about to achieve equivalent status, or as a prime minister of a sovereign state in proper standing and one representing an illicit regime approaching a deserved extinction? The answer was ambiguous. Some of the terms related to Rhodesia's future as an independent polity. The existing regime in Rhodesia would not be permitted to survive to negotiate the terms in specifics, but it was given a prospectus on the basis of which to yield its existence and to renounce rebellion. The rest of the terms pertained to arrangements for governing Rhodesia in the sequel to capitulation, a return to legality, as put by the British.

Another start was to be made on a constitution, with the 1961 text as a base. Formal executive power would be as before, though with a governor general appointed on Rhodesia's nomination. Active executive power would be arranged as before. Legislative power would be in a two-house legislature. An assembly would have sixty-seven members from three sorts of overlapping single-member constituencies apportioned on a country-wide basis. Separate voting lists corresponding to the higher and lower qualifications already existing would be preserved. All indigenous citizens more than thirty years old, unless on the higher-qualified list, would be added to the lower. Thirty-three seats would be allotted to higher-qualified constituencies and seventeen to lower. Seventeen seats would be reserved to white voters exclusively. A Senate of twenty-six would be added, with twelve seats assigned to constituencies consisting of white voters in the higher qualification, eight to constituencies of indigenous voters irrespective of qualification, and six to chiefs chosen by tribal hierarchies. The Senate would be coordinate in general legislation and pre-eminent on tribal affairs. Entrenched clauses of the constitution would be amendable by vote of three-fourths of both houses voting together. Any amendment of the bill of rights or one involving racial discrimination would be subject to appeal to the Rhodesian constitutional commission and, beyond it, to the Judicial Committee of the Privy Council in London.

The terms concerning a return to legality were linked to a stipulation for determination of the acceptability of the prospective constitution to the

Rhodesian population as a whole as a step antecedent to introduction of necessary legislation in the British Parliament. A commission would work out and apply a method. Its composition would be decided between the British government and a successor Rhodesian regime. If the commission should elicit an affirmative answer, the interim provisions would probably be in effect only briefly. A negative determination might leave them in effect indefinitely. For the interim, whatever its duration, the British government would take a directing role in Rhodesia's affairs. Authority would be effectuated, rather than merely personified, through a London-appointed governor. He would be vested with operative control, as distinguished from formal command, over Rhodesia's armed forces. As such, he would be advised by a council consisting of certain ministers, heads of the component services, and, notably, an additional representative of the British government. Subject only to a stipulation for initially reappointing Rhodesia's prime minister of the time, the governor would name ministers in his own discretion. Local executive accountability would be ended by this provision and by a provision for immediate dissolution of the legislature. Instead, accountability would be to London. Perfecting of details would be left to a regime thus constituted for the interim and the British government. The latter would still have, as legal instruments at hand, its order-in-council and the act of Parliament passed in the immediate aftermath of Rhodesia's move for independence. Thus unequivocally, for an interim, Rhodesia would be reduced to a Crown colony's status, which it had never had before. Temporarily anyway, it would become non-self-governing.

The British government commended itself for generous terms. The configurations for a new constitution appeared indeed to represent a considerable movement away from former positions and from what was implied by Britain's alignment, through a Security Council resolution, with the General Assembly's 1960 prescription of terms for decolonization and independence. To that degree, they approached the Rhodesian regime's views. Despite misgivings about some details, the Rhodesian regime concurred in them. The sticking points were in the conditions for return to legality. To the Rhodesians, right or wrong, these amounted to measures of a defeat which Great Britain had singularly failed to inflict— a subordination at variance with Rhodesia's past. On that premise, under the time pressure of an ultimatum, and against a background of eroded trust between the parties to negotiation, the terms were rejected. Perhaps it was a case, as *The Wall Street Journal* observed, of a "good deal of misplaced pride" on both sides. Following the rejection, the British government renounced all offers. Thenceforth so it avowed, the only acceptable basis for independence would be general enfranchisement of the indigenous population. Such had been the Labour Party's position on the matter before its advent to office. Such were the terms demanded in a succession of General Assembly resolutions and finally by a Security Council resolution, all based on a premise regarding Rhodesia as non-self-governing.

In form of a law empowering it to take all needful measures, the British government had available, on paper, all authority necessary to the aim. Besides its existing order-in-council, Britain could issue other decrees conceivably required for realizing the purpose now articulated. The paper aspects of policy are the easiest. Giving effect to the aims would be another matter. As if to exemplify the difficulty, Britain, after having explicitly assumed all governance over Rhodesia, still withheld registering Rhodesia as a non-self-governing territory, because it confronted a circumstance previously explained to an unheeding General Assembly—namely, a lack of access to data on which to base required reports. Britain lacked the data because in fact it did not govern Rhodesia.

In obdurate fact, and in face of hostility proclaimed by much of the world, Rhodesia was self-governing. How well was it managing? The censorship accompanying its beleaguerement made a definitive answer difficult. A correspondent of London's *Economist* reported evidences of economic and political security in Rhodesia, an upsurge in manufactures, a money market awash with liquidity. On a basis of confidences from bureaucrats in London's Commonwealth Relations Office, Russell Warren Howe, in *The Baltimore Sun,* reported inexorable decline and approaching collapse. *Fortune*'s John Davenport found a tranquil countryside and busy industries. He concluded: ". . . the more the outside world threatens Rhodesia, the greater will become its will to keep the economy moving today, and indeed to expand its development for tomorrow." *The Washington Post*'s Donald Louchheim summed up a "stunning victory" after a year of what the world called illegal independence. Economic sanctions and diplomatic ostracism notwithstanding, he described Rhodesia as "one of the strongest, most stable new nations in Africa." He added: "British prestige and credibility have received staggering blows. Black

Africa's impotence has been starkly revealed." He concluded: "From every point of view, independence is an accomplished fact. Despite threats of new, sterner sanctions, nothing short of military force seems likely to alter it." Circumstances may, or may not, have been as favorable as the Rhodesian minister of finance made out in reporting to his Parliament a drop of less than 5 percent in gross domestic product in 1966 compared to 1965, but on balance they seemed hugely more favorable than the authors of sanctions had anticipated.

Great Britain put hope in somehow worsening Rhodesia's circumstances to the extent necessary to compel submission to Britain's revised stipulations made after Rhodesia's rejection of the terms for a return to legality. Britain sought another Security Council resolution calling for sterner deprivations in a more peremptory voice. This time the aim was to make the pattern of sanctions binding on all member governments rather than, as previously, a matter of voluntary cooperation. This appeared to be a case of shifting the point of reference in the Charter from Chapter VI to Chapter VII. Under the Charter's terms, the aim could be achieved only in event of a threat to the peace, a breach of the peace, or an act of aggression, but the initial British draft did not cite any of these contingencies. Another delegate inquired as to the basis for the sterner action called for. By general assent, a threat to the peace was averred, and the phrase was inserted to bring the action into verbal consonance with the Charter. It was an averment without much apparent conviction. Later on, a question of the basis of action was asked in the House of Commons, and the British prime minister said that it could be interpreted as something between Chapter VI and Chapter VII.

WHAT THREAT TO WHAT PEACE?

International law does not proclaim the sanctity of British dominion over palm and pine. Certainly we Americans are in no position to declare it—we who conspired to instigate French aggression against British power in America and not only threatened but shattered international peace to achieve our independence.—Dean Acheson

"Freedom when men act in groups is power," Edmund Burke observed in a simple comment on institutions. By an obvious corollary, the idea holds true when groups act in combination. Power, according to a famous cliché, tends to corrupt—meaning that those vested with capacity to direct others are prone to come to view this capacity as an end in itself. In short, power has a dynamic of its own, and those who possess it may become possessed by it. That is why institutions need limitative rules to constrain them to the purposes for which they have been founded and procedural rules to help prevent them from overrunning their assigned limits. They must operate under ordinances both to keep them confined to their proper scope even when they adhere to proper procedure and to ensure that they follow proper procedure when acting within that scope. Such matters cannot be ensured solely by the letter of rules, for they are matters of spirit. Yet a respect for prescribed rules is surely essential to the preservation of rectitude, just as a careless attitude toward rules conduces to decay. Such copybook maxims have a bearing on the United Nations' role.

The organization, however, has uncritical devotees who incline to view it as epitomizing in all aspects and operations the lofty purposes set forth in the Charter. To that outlook, good is pervasive and inherent in the organization itself so that benefit inheres in whatever the organization does or becomes. Change is equated with flourishing. Dynamism in the organization inevitably tends toward improvement and is therefore to be welcomed and affirmed. Practice is paramount over precept. When some action undertaken does not accord with the Charter's prescription, it is explained as an instance of "developing the Charter."

To a contrasting view—my own is akin to it rather than to the former—the organization deserves the respect of having its activities subjected to the exacting scrutiny and critical judgment which in all large undertakings are indispensable to the preservation of standards. Prevailing practice is not necessarily a warrant for its own justification. To the contrary, as Sir Percy Spender expressed the point while serving as Judge on the International Court of Justice, "Unless it is of a peaceful, uniform, and undisputed character, practice has no probative value." Where others might see an action as "developing the Charter," holders of this second view would more likely discern abuse of the Charter. To this view, change may represent deterioration as well as progress. All acts of governments, taken alone or in concert, are likely to be the better for being occasionally exposed to skeptical examination. An action by a collectivity of governments is not necessarily better than an action by a single one. On the contrary, the processes of what is called collective diplomacy abound with special temptations to forensic display. Pressures may distort deliberation. There may be irresponsibility as well as safety in numbers. Accordingly, it is all the more important to judge the forum by the quality of decisions rather than to evaluate decisions according to the forum. Just as the former view is likely to value dynamism in construing the United Nations' proper role, so the latter view is likely to put emphasis on the original precepts. It keeps in mind that the pledge of good faith in performance of obligations, linked by the progenitors of the Charter to the right and putative benefits resulting from membership, is susceptible of being forsaken by a preponderance of members as well as by one or two at a time, and that the pledge is directed to "the present Charter," the literal document.

Debate over United Nations policy toward Rhodesia, heightened by the two Security Council actions of 1966 citing a threat to the peace, has polarized around the two contrasting views of organization in relation to the Charter's precise terms. The relevant provisions show clear awareness, on the part of the Charter's authors, of a need for establishing bounds to the powers authorized. This is specifically so with respect to the great potential of Chapter VII. The Security Council, consisting of five permanent and initially of six and more recently of ten members serving in rotation, is, within limits for matters of peace and security, endowed with authority akin to that of a world government. Stress here is on the limits. In Leland S. Goodrich's words, it "not only is given 'primary responsibility' for maintaining international peace and security but also is under specific instructions as to how it may and should proceed in discharging that responsibility." Any invocation of mandatory powers is made contingent upon a favorable vote of two-thirds, including the concurring votes of the permanent members. The circumstances warranting invocation of its mandatory powers are specified as threats to the peace, breaches of the peace, and acts of aggression. The powers are subordinated to a provision, in paragraph 7 of Article 2, that "Nothing contained in the present Charter shall authorize the United Nations to intervene in matters which are essentially within the domestic jurisdiction of any state or shall require the Members to submit such matters to settlement under the present Charter; but the principle shall not prejudice the application of enforcement measures under Chapter VII."

Attempts at justification of the controverted actions have relied on the following interwoven propositions. The purpose in view, namely compulsion of an immediate change of the basis of government in Rhodesia to an indigenous majority, is desirable as a principle. Also, supporting it garners good will and avoids alienation among the numerous new independencies of Africa. Dissatisfaction among Rhodesia's northerly neighbors is sufficient to present a putative probability of violence at some subsequent stage, and therefore to constitute a threat to the peace. Lack of statehood in Rhodesia places its domestic affairs beyond the protection afforded by paragraph 7 of Article 2. Since Great Britain as the administering power over Rhodesia invited the actions concerned, the actions are by definition not interventions. The protection of domestic affairs against United Nations intervention is, by its own terms, not applicable when enforcement action under Chapter VII is being invoked. Anyway, a question of the existence of a threat to the peace and of action required to counter it is one solely for the Security Council to decide, and its decisions are beyond challenge. These arguments are not cogent.

The point about desirability of purpose is certainly supportable in abstract terms. A good many people support it. By habit and sentiment, Americans subscribe to precepts of majority rule. Apologists for sanctions against Rhodesia are wont to invoke the Declaration of Independence in support of this position. The document at the foundation of the United States' national existence did state a universal proposition about human equality and linked the just powers of governments to consent of the governed. On May 26, 1966, the President voiced these ideas in a speech touching specifically on Rhodesia:

> The foreign policy of the United States is rooted in its life at home. We will not permit human rights to be restricted in our own country. And we will not support policies abroad which are based on the rule of minorities or the discredited notion that men are unequal before the law.
>
> We will not live by a double standard—professing abroad what we do not practice at home, or venerating at home what we ignore abroad.

He referred to "self-determination and an orderly transition to majority rule in every quarter of the globe" as principles which "guide our policy toward Rhodesia." He said that the United States could not "condone the perpetuation of racial or political injustice anywhere in the world."

On the other hand, in clear acknowledgment of inequality among cultures, the Declaration of Independence also inveighed against George III for having loosed "merciless savage Indians" against his subjects. It mitigated its universal propositions with an "appeal to consanguinity." At the onset of Amer-

ican independence the franchise was limited to a
small portion of American adult white males, qualified on a basis of property and income. The Declaration did not enfranchise females or any non-whites
whatever, elevate any Indians, or emancipate a single
slave. The realization of America's rightly vaunted
equality and wide participation in public affairs took
much time and effort and even yet does not proceed
without disorder. It is well enough to inveigh against
a double standard that distinguishes between matters abroad and those at home. Yet independence
for any nation, and peace and order among them all,
rest on respect for double standards in the sense
that no state is entitled to prescribe for others and
to impose its own standards beyond its own span of
jurisdiction. That is the principle given classic expression by Emerich de Vattel: "No sovereign
state may inquire into the manner in which a sovereign rules nor set itself up as a judge of his conduct
nor force him to make any change in his administration. If he burdens his subjects with taxes or treats
them with severity, it is for the nation to take action; no foreign state is called on to mend his conduct and to force him to follow a wiser and juster
course." The makers of the Charter wisely reflected
that principle in paragraph 7 of Article 2, making
clear that what international law forbade to states
acting singly was not to be justified merely by making the action collective. Other parts of the Charter
guiding the organization are permissive, contingent,
and discretionary, but the precept concerned is cate-
gorical. It is, in Dean Acheson's phrase, "the one
law of the United Nations." One does not clear the
barrier by asserting desirability for the purpose
sought to be imposed. All interventions are deemed

desirable by the proponents. The Charter's language does not make an exception for ends deemed desirable and ban only those interventions which may be proposed for purposes without appealing qualities, for that would amount to having no prohibition whatever.

In any event, a forcing of immediate wholesale enfranchisement of the indigenous population in Rhodesia is not demonstrably a step toward the desideratum referred to in the President's cited remarks as "orderly transition." Writing in *The New York Times,* Arthur Krock has expressed the doubt bluntly: "The dismal, incontrovertible proof in some emerging African states that . . . 'violence and chaos' have attended the establishment of 'non-white majority rule,' fairly exposes the policy of the Wilson Government to attack as dynamite loaded sentimentality with a fast fuse." In a similar vein, "The basic issue is how soon political equality in citizenship can be established without the destruction in Rhodesia, by the compound of sentimentality and expediency in the foreign policy of London and Washington, of those values which the policy has destroyed elsewhere in Africa." The Rhodesian regime has professed to have no regressive intentions regarding the pace of developing the indigenous majority for political participation. Conjecturally, that regime might harbor such intentions, and the dominant minority might be expected to become increasingly reluctant as its loss of ascendency moved from being a remote to an imminent prospect. The regime, however, has not balked at giving guarantees regarding maintenance of a steady pace of transition. Despite the authors' intentions, the policy of economic deprivation against Rhodesia seems a certain way of retarding that pace by impinging on opportunity for improved livelihood and resources for education within Rhodesia. To support this improvident undertaking by asserting its appeal to some of Rhodesia's neighbors, who may repay favor with good will, is to mortgage policy to public relations and to subjugate a great power's judgment in grave affairs to the whims of necessitous neophyte nations.

Dissatisfactions among Rhodesia's neighbors and a corollary possibility of general violence at some stage are postulates deserving examination. These are the elements cited to substantiate allegations of a threat to the peace and thus to justify actions under Chapter VII of the Charter. As a point for emphasis, supporters of the policy do not ordinarily attribute aggressive intentions toward Rhodesia itself. True, a General Assembly resolution in November, 1965, did allege "threats made by the present authorities in Southern Rhodesia, including a threat of economic sabotage against the independent African states adjoining," but it adduced no supporting evidence. The usual hypothesis, however, is that Rhodesia's neighbors are the ones that may launch impermissible violence on a substantial scale. Dean Acheson has appraised the logic of invoking this line of argument in support of the policy pursued:

> Since Rhodesia, by doing what it has always done and with which the United Nations cannot constitutionally interfere, incites less law-abiding members to violate their solemn obligation not to use force or the threat of force in their international relations, Rhodesia becomes a threat to the peace and must be coerced.

Mr. Acheson's conclusion is: "If this reasoning leads the reader to ask . . .'Who's loony now?' don't blame

Rhodesia, blame the Security Council and Harold Wilson."

The concept of threat to the peace deserves elucidation in this connection. A threat is not merely an inferred possibility of an occurrence which might conceivably take place under hypothetical conditions. It must be articulated as a demonstrable probability. The dictionary meaning is "the expression of an intention to inflict evil or injury on another," and an intention must encompass not only a wish but also putative means for giving it effect. Such are its meanings in law. If one were to go into court seeking a restraining order against someone's threat and in support were to allege unsubstantiated possibilities unsupported by demonstrable means, the high probability is that the court would dismiss the plea out of hand. In stipulating a threat to the peace as a condition for invoking the Security Council's compulsory powers under Chapter VII, the progenitors of the Charter were using language advisedly. The aim was a narrow, not a limitless, authorization. The globe abounds with situations which do not accord with the preferences of one government or another, and which, under hypothetical conditions, might be productive of violence. To construe the pertinent phrase in Chapter VII as a warrant for the Security Council to invoke compulsory action on behalf of those who, because of frustrated preferences, might conceivably resort to force is to infer for the United Nations a mission to engender unending hostilities. The idea is antithetic to the Charter's main purpose as a framework of principles promotive of peace. The case for broadly construing the meaning of threat to the peace in this instance may be countered with an equally persuasive point, as expressed in *The*

Wall Street Journal: "The argument for sanctions is that they may force southern Africa to drop racialism before an explosion of Africans ignites the continent. Yet any escalation of those sanctions may set off an equally dangerous explosion and may do so far earlier than any trouble that might develop if Africa were left to its own resources."

The premise denying Rhodesia's statehood and the inference placing it outside the protection of domestic jurisdiction under paragraph 7 of Article 2 of the Charter are closely linked to the proposition that the actions concerned are not interventions because Great Britain, as administering power, invited the Security Council to take them. These assertions are merely nominalistic retreats from substantive difficulties. They seek to avoid grave issues of policy by invoking terms of art. By the unarticulated premise, facts are to be determined by the names applied. In policy, the sound approach is to choose terminology to fit the facts. The proposition holding statehood to be integral to recognition as a state by antecedent states invites a question of how the first state to exist ever managed to materialize. References in context to Great Britain as administering power invite a counter observation that, if the designation be correct, then the problem of Rhodesia vanishes.

One should keep in mind Professor D. P. O'Connell's warning, in his *International Law,* that "the inclusion or exclusion of any particular entity from the category of 'State' cannot be presumed from any *a priori* notion of the qualifications of Statehood." The relevant provision of the Charter, consonant with the pre-eminent aim of fostering peace, was designed as a protection of domestic jurisdiction. It was not designed as a point of reference for arguing about technicalities of definition. In any event, the principle prevailing in international law has been that expressed in the Montevideo Convention on the Rights and Duties of States, defining qualifications for statehood as possession of a permanent population, a defined territory, government, and capacity to enter into relations with other states. By long-established criteria Rhodesia appears to qualify.

The proposition seeking to except Rhodesia from the ban on intervention in matters within a state's domestic jurisdiction has been supported by an assertion that "the record shows that the United Nations, over the years, has also recognized Southern Rhodesia as falling within the provisions of Chapter XI of the Charter"—to wit, a non-self-governing area. True, that has been the gist of General Assembly resolutions over a five-year period. The argument, quoted from the United States spokesman's presentation in the Security Council's deliberations, leaves out of account Great Britain's persistent denial of the assumption, the United States' consistent support of the denial, and Great Britain's continued lack of access to data for making relevant reports to the United Nations. Another proposition in support is, as given in an address by the State Department's assistant secretary for African affairs, "that Britain always reserved constitutionally the right to veto any discriminatory legislation directed at the indigenous population, and that Britain never yielded these rights." Whatever its theoretic relevance, the point is factually not correct. Britain did in fact yield its veto power over Rhodesian legislation in the 1961 constitution.

The argument focusing on the provisions of paragraph 7 of Article 2 of the Charter holding that any invocation of enforcement action overrides the restriction against intervention in matters essentially within a state's domestic jurisdiction has already been dealt with indirectly, but some additional observations are in order. Credulity is strained by an interpretation holding the language to license by implication the very thing it explicitly forbids. The relation between the two elements of the paragraph is plain enough when read with care and in relation to Chapter VII. The reservation against prejudicing the application of enforcement action is not a grant of jurisdiction. It refers only to the propriety of instrumentalities in instances where substantive jurisdiction is properly founded. As an illustration, the Security Council, in ordering interdictions against a state validly found to have been threatening or breaching the peace or committing aggression, may go so far as to ban payments in performance on private insurance contracts even though performance on such contracts belongs within domestic jurisdiction. The fallacy of interpreting the reservation to contradict the language preceding it may be demonstrated by a rough analogy. Imagine an instance of a municipality establishing a fire department. The authorities take into account the importance of ensuring against mischievous use of the personnel and equipment and therefore specify a ban against their interposition to run people's personal affairs and domestic activities. They add a prudent reservation against interpreting the ban to inhibit the fire company's effectiveness in dealing with real fires. Notwithstanding the restriction, the firemen intrude into a domestic situation and justify the act by a claim of having taken care first to ring the alarm bell.

An argument finally to be appraised is that asserting the conclusiveness of the Security Council's jurisdiction and findings. The argument does not meet the issue. The Security Council's place as the authority of primary responsibility designated by the Charter is not in question. What is in question is the wisdom with which it has used that authority. Unfortunately, the record forming the basis of its action does not have the attribute of conclusiveness. It is not a thorough record. The evidence adduced to support conclusions is refractory and one-sided. That result was inherent in the Security Council's decision to deny Rhodesia opportunity for contesting the case and to act only on the basis of hearing one side, a decision linked to the denial to Rhodesia of any putative standing as a state. The decision was at variance with a long list of precedents related to disputes involving entities without standing as states.

The conclusiveness of the Security Council's actions, moreover, involves a question related to voting requirements. The affirmative majorities in each of the resolutions invoking authority under Chapter VII did not include two of the permanent members, namely France and the Soviet Union, both abstaining. A practice of convenience, strongly encouraged by the United States itself, is that of regarding an abstention as without effect in relation to the Charter provision requiring the concurring votes of permanent members for substantive actions. It counts an abstention as a withholding of opposition and therefore as being akin to concurrence. The usage is supported by an inference drawn from the circumstance that the language concerned refers only to "the permanent members"—conceivably meaning the ones casting votes rather than the sum total of permanent members. The rub is that in the Charter versions other than English a term meaning "all" is included in the provision in question. Time and choice seem to have eroded a requirement explicit in the Charter. Yet the instant examples raise grave doubts. These may be illustrated by the French representative's declaration incident to the vote on interdicting tankers—"In these circumstances, my delegation cannot associate itself with any text that seeks to affirm that there exists a threat to the peace." It strains credulity to construe a concurring vote from so explicit a nonconcurring non-vote. The point has special pertinence because in these instances, unlike those of the past, the intent is to make the Security Council's actions mandatory on reluctant states.

In sum, one finds in the record evidence of questionable procedure and superficiality in substance. Great decisions made in such fashion almost inevitably produce unintended results and all too often confound the purposes toward which action is directed. Such has been the case respecting Rhodesia until now.

I discussed the prospect with an able and forthcoming political leader from one of Africa's neophyte states. Trying to restore a disintegrated political situation and to bolster a flagging economy were tasks enough for his own country, he said. Officially, for a calculable future, his government would support enfranchisement of Rhodesia's black majority, but of more pressing importance was the fact that his own countrymen had not yet experienced a free election in their own land. A proper constitution for Rhodesia was a good idea, but his own country had no constitution whatever in effect at the moment. Rhodesia was not going to attack its neighbors, and none of them could attack Rhodesia. The great powers had taken over the whole problem. They, and especially the United States, were the ones to handle Rhodesia. In the Security Council they had declared Rhodesia a threat to the peace. The Security Council could not give that status to the problem and then wash its hands of it. If the present pattern of sanctions should not succeed in bringing down the Rhodesian regime, armed action must be undertaken to enforce them. That would be a task for those commanding the necessary resources. They would be reminded of their responsibilities to act accordingly in due time, he said. I discussed the prospect also with friends in Congress, in the State Department, in the Department of Defense, and on the President's staff. Unanimously, they disclaimed any intention, and all possibility, of United States military involvement.

Trouble is likely to emerge from the gap between those contrasting sets of expectations. One can only trust that it will never grow too late for thorough thought and, as necessary, for some backtracking on an issue in which there is so little likelihood of doing good and so much of making matters worse.

My counsel is not for faithlessness to obligations in the realm of the United Nations. To the contrary, what the United States must do is to point the way to proper use of the Charter. That course would not involve disservice to Africa's burgeoning new states. Rather, it would mark an end to the unwise practice of humoring them in exorbitant designs.

Nor would it be a case of letting down an old ally. When Great Britain was in need of cautionary advice against asserting purposes beyond its means in regard to Rhodesia, the United States government did not say the saving word it could have said. When the British government, tentatively recovering perspective, resumed communication with the Rhodesian regime in the spring of 1966, the President of the United States regrettably voiced implicit disapproval. When Great Britain, pushed to extremity by compounded failures, sought mandatory sanctions, the United States, given wisdom enough, could have averted folly with a veto in the Security Council. Instead, it chose to collude in the fallacious course. The next opportunity to aid a baffled friend must not be muffed.

Elspeth Huxley has ably expounded that last theme. Her plea begins with a reminder that "the pace of African political advancement, the only serious issue," had been "more or less agreed upon." What gave rise to crisis in the latter stage of the dispute was quite another matter. Britain's insistence on an act of capitulation at variance with Rhodesia's history was ranged against Rhodesia's assertion of independence on its own initiative, "without waiting for one of Britain's royal family to come and haul down the Union Jack and hoist another flag, an occupation that has kept them on the hop in recent years." The regime must therefore be destroyed as illegal. "It is this that bothers Mr. Wilson," Mrs. Huxley observes. Her appeal concludes:

> We in Britain cannot now extricate ourselves from the mess. We are on the escalator, going down, and there's something nasty in the basement. The United States is about the only hope we have. If it could persuade Mr. Wilson to snap out of his imperialist dreams of flags, rebels, governors, oaths of allegiance, and so forth, there is no reason why a reasonable compromise, that would secure

the political advancement of Rhodesia's Africans without first obliging them to starve to death, could not be reached.

Policy is out on a limb. An account of how it got there will serve its purpose if it helps arouse concern for finding a way back from predicament.